GOD'S WORD

FOR

Every Need

DESTINY IMAGE® PUBLISHERS, INC.
P.O. Box 310, Shippensburg, PA 17257-0310
"Promoting Inspired Lives."

This book and all other Destiny Image and Destiny Image Fiction books are available at Christian bookstores and distributors worldwide.

Cover design by Eileen Rockwell
Interior design by Terry Clifton

For more information on foreign distributors, call
717-532-3040.
Or reach us on the Internet: www.destinyimage.com

ISBN 13: 978-0-7684-1040-2

For Worldwide Distribution, Printed in China
1 2 3 4 5 6 7 8 9 10 11 /18 17 16 15

~ *God's Word* ~

If ever there was a time when we needed ancient, timeless wisdom to help us navigate the challenges of life it is today. With the institutions and systems of the world being so obviously shaken, people are looking more and more for fixed points in a changing and sometimes unsettling universe.

This is why the God's Word series of small gift books is so timely. The Bible contains wisdom and truth that has stood the test of time. It continues to be the world's bestselling book and the volume that most people reach for when the storms of life strike.

The words of the Bible startle us with their relevance because its ultimate author stands above and beyond time and yet reaches out to His children within time and speaks with a heart of love to them, guiding them through troubled waters, comforting them in the shipwrecks of life.

There is quite simply no other book on the planet that speaks into our day-to-day lives like this book.

As you open the pages of *God's Word for Every Need*, don't think of the words you're about to read as a catalogue of rules and regulations from a harsh and distant God. Think of them as phrases and sentences from the longest love letter in history. Think of them as soothing whispers from a living, loving God.

The Bible is not a legal tome. It is a love letter from heaven to earth, from our Heavenly Father to His beloved children.

So don't be deceived. *God's Word for Every Need* may be a small book but it will have a great impact if you let it.

God is about to speak to your needs.

Open your ears and your heart.

Let the Father's tender voice transform your life.

Contents

Acceptance

The moment Jesus came up out of the baptismal waters, the skies opened up and he saw God's Spirit—it looked like a dove—descending and landing on him. And along with the Spirit, a voice: "This is my Son, chosen and marked by my love, delight of my life."

MATTHEW 3:16–17

When Jesus was baptized, He came up out of the waters and received the Father's acceptance. The heavens were opened and He heard His Father say, "You're my Son. I love you. You're the delight of my life." This is something we can all hear. When we choose to follow Jesus, we are filled with the Holy Spirit. Christ is then in us and we are in Christ. If we are in Christ, then we can stand in the river with Him. We can stand with Him and in Him under an open heaven. In Jesus we can hear the Father speak to us, "You're my child. I love you. You're the delight of my life." This is the foundation of everything. We do not work *for* God's acceptance. We work *from* it. The Father accepts all those who are in Christ. He not only accepts us, He affirms us and even applauds us because it is first and foremost our position not our performance that causes His heart to sing.

Answers

Trust God from the bottom of your heart; don't try to figure out everything on your own. Listen for God's voice in everything you do, everywhere you go; He's the one who will keep you on track.

PROVERBS 3:5–6

There are times in our lives when we need answers. Maybe we are going through a season where our faith is being sorely tested, perhaps by challenging circumstances or by cynical questions. Maybe we are facing some very tough decisions about our future, or the future of a loved one. Whenever this happens, the greatest obstacle to finding answers is our self-reliance. When this happens we are like those who drive round and round a town for hours when a simple question to a passer-by would lead us to our destination. Our independence is our downfall. We want to work it out for ourselves and manage on our own. If we have this mindset, God challenges us to lean correctly. If we lean on our own intellects, answers will elude us. If we lean on Him, as a child on their parent, then we will hear the answers. It's all a matter of childlike leaning and attentive listening! When we position ourselves to hear God, He will keep us on track.

Assurance

*God assured us, "I'll never let you
down, never walk off and leave you."*
HEBREWS 13:5

If you have ever been abandoned by someone you loved deeply, you'll know that one of the hardest things is to trust someone again. A deep-seated fear can paralyze you into not making any kind of commitment to another person in your world because you are afraid that history will repeat itself and you'll be deserted again. This is totally understandable but it is also totally reversible. God understands why we feel that way but He also knows how to help us to trust again. The good news is that God is not like earthly mothers and fathers who abandon their children. He is the Dad who never forsakes His kids. He is the Husband who never deserts His bride. He alone is 100 percent trustworthy and when He promises that He will never walk off and leave us, He truly means it and we can truly believe it. So let His assurance fill your heart and heal your wounds today.

Boldness

> *While they were praying, the place where they were meeting trembled and shook. They were all filled with the Holy Spirit and continued to speak God's Word with fearless confidence.*
>
> ACTS 4:31

Peter and John had stood up to the intimidation of the religious leaders in Jerusalem who had told them not to speak any more about Jesus. Peter and John refused. Having been released, they went back to their fellow believers and they all began to pray for boldness. God heard their prayer and gave them a fresh outpouring of the Holy Spirit. This gave them "fearless confidence" in speaking God's Word and in turn gave us an abiding example for when we need boldness. All we have to do is refuse to bow under the intimidation of the enemy. We must bow only before our Father in heaven and ask for that ability to speak the name of Jesus with unwavering confidence. If your prayer is for boldness to speak about Jesus, rest assured God will give you what you need. He will fill you with fresh certainty that Jesus has the name above all other names.

Bravery

"Haven't I commanded you? Strength!
Courage! Don't be timid; don't get
discouraged. God, your God, is
with you every step you take."

JOSHUA 1:8–9

Sometimes in our lives, we are called to make big decisions. At such moments we can be overcome by the fear of failure, humiliation, poverty, and of course pain. When this happens, we need to remember that bravery does not consist in the elimination of fear but in the management of it. No one who has shown exceptional courage has been without fear. They have simply learned how to master it well. Joshua needed to be brave when crossing the borders into the Promised Land, a place where giants roamed. Gods didn't anaesthetize or remove Joshua's fears. He spoke a word that enabled Joshua to conquer his fears. So often the real giants are not in the land, they are in our hearts. God's Word is simple: "I am with you every step of the way." If we are walking in His will, He is with us. If He is with us, who can stand against us? Whatever the big decision is in your life right now, be brave. Master your fear through the application of God's magnificent promises.

Breakthrough

> "*Then I, God, will burst all confinements and lead them out into the open.*
> *They'll follow their King.*
> *I will be out in front leading them.*"
> MICAH 2:13

Most of us have known the experience of being confined at one time or another in our lives. Maybe we have felt hemmed in by a particular place. Maybe we have felt trapped and boxed in by a particular set of circumstances. Maybe we have felt obstructed by a lack of resources, human or material. Maybe we have felt restricted by those opposing our advance. If the future we desire conforms to the will of God, then we have every confidence when we go in prayer to the God of the Breakthrough. God is not only our loving Father who wants the best for us. He is also our mighty King who knows how to bring that best into being. He is the Breaker who knows how to burst through the walls that restrict us. When we look to Him and prevail in prayer, He will help us to break out of our confinements and enter those wide and open spaces where we can thrive

Certainty

*From now on, whatever you request along
the lines of who I am and what I am doing,
I'll do it. That's how the Father will be
seen for who he is in the Son. I mean it.
Whatever you request in this way, I'll do.*

John 14:13–14

How can we be certain that what we are asking for in prayer will be answered by God with a "Yes?" Here Jesus promises His disciples that whatever they ask for "in His name" will be answered favorably. Does that mean we can be sure of answered prayer if we simply add "in Jesus' name" to it? No, that is not what Jesus meant. In His day and in His culture, a person's name was their character and their character was their name. To pray in Jesus' name therefore meant to pray "in line with Jesus' character." To us it means "to pray in a way that Jesus would pray." Whenever we make a request for any need that is in alignment with who Jesus is and what Jesus does, then we can be sure that the answer is, "Yes, I'll do it!" We can pray with certainty when we pray with consistency—in a way that is consistent with who Jesus is.

Clarity

God will make it all plain.
2 TIMOTHY 2:7

Sometimes our minds can become muddled and our wills undecided. When this happens we need to remember that God does not lead us into confusion but into peace. He doesn't give us clouded judgments and an uneasy heart but a clear direction and a peaceful spirit. If you don't experience His peace over an issue, then the chances are your mind is out of sync with His mind. Once your thinking is aligned with His thinking (as revealed in His Word), then your thoughts will be clear and your decisions sound. So renew your mind in the Word and the Spirit. Make sure that your will is properly in sync with His will. As you do, your loving Father will make it all plain. You will go from feeling troubled to being at ease in His presence and at peace with your decisions. You will go from obscurity to clarity.

Cleansing

If we admit our sins—make a clean breast of them—he won't let us down; he'll be true to himself. He'll forgive our sins and purge us of all wrongdoing.
1 John 1:8–9

Sometimes the effects of sin can leave us feeling dirty and ashamed. We come to God with repentant hearts, asking for His forgiveness. We sense that we are forgiven but we still feel as if the stains of what we've done, or what's been done to us, affect and mar our lives. The beautiful thing about God's amazing grace is that He promises not only to remove the sin itself but the effects of that sin in our lives. When we repent, He forgives and He removes our sin as far from us as the east is from the west. That's great. But there's even greater! When we are truly honest before Him, our loving Heavenly Father not only promises to forgive. He also promises to purge and cleanse us of all wrongdoing. What glorious good news that is! Our Father not only forgives; He cleanses. He not only purges us of *some* wrongdoing; He purges us of *all* wrongdoing. Why not wash in His cleansing streams today?

Closure

God guards you from every evil, he
guards your very life. He guards you
when you leave and when you return, he
guards you now, he guards you always.

PSALM 121:7–8

Between one season ending and another starting it can be very challenging. The time between endings and beginnings often demands a great deal from us. One of the most important things to do is make sure you bring closure to the old season. Ask God to guard and protect your leave-taking. If that's a job or a ministry, ask Him to empower you to leave well. If it's a relationship, ask Him to help you to say your goodbyes in the right way and at the right time. Life is full of leave-taking, most of it of a relatively painless kind. Sometimes, however, we have to say bigger and tougher goodbyes. The more we allow our Heavenly Father to guard and bless our leaving, the more He will bless our entering. So ask your Heavenly Father to meet your need for closure today. Resolve to leave the old season under His blessing so that you can start the new one under it too.

Comfort

All praise to the God and Father of our Master, Jesus the Messiah! Father of all mercy! God of all healing counsel! He comes alongside us when we go through hard times, and before you know it, he brings us alongside someone else who is going through hard times so that we can be there for that person just as God was there for us.
2 Corinthians 1:3

One of the greatest things about our Heavenly Father is the way He can make a testimony out of our testing. Many times God allows us to go through difficult times so that we can experience a comfort that is tailor-made to those circumstances. Once we have received that comfort we are then in an unprecedented and unparalleled position to bring that same comfort to those going through the same experience. This is why we often find that drug addicts, having been saved and delivered by God, go back as ambassadors of God's freedom into the drug-addicted community. They are uniquely positioned to bring God's comfort because they themselves have experienced it. The same is true for prisoners, for victims of abuse, for the bereaved, and so on. Having been comforted, they then become carriers of this comfort to those who are yet to encounter the soothing love of God. Receive the healing counsel of the Father today and then get alongside those who are still walking the road that you once walked.

Companionship

*My father and mother walked out
and left me, but God took me in.*

PSALM 27:10

Sooner or later in our lives, we are left behind by those we love. This can happen in all sorts of ways—death, divorce, desertion, to name just a few. If you have been abandoned by your father, or your mother, or anyone whom you loved, this verse from Psalm 27 is a great comfort. When others walk out on us, our Father stays put. When others leave us homeless, He takes us in. When others withdraw their affection, He holds us close. Our Father is steadfast and true, faithful and loving. If you have any kind of grief in your life right now, trust Him. Let Him heal your hurts and restore your life. He will never leave you nor forsake you. He has promised to be with you until the end of time. While others may prove to be unfaithful, He is forever faithful. Let that great and unshakable truth console your heart and bring hope to your life.

Confidence

"Embrace this God-life. Really embrace it, and nothing will be too much for you. This mountain, for instance: Just say, 'Go jump in the lake'—no shuffling or shilly-shallying—and it's as good as done."

MARK 11:22–23

Every so often we are confronted by what Jesus describes as a "mountain." What did He mean by that? A mountain is anything that masquerades as an impossible situation in your life. It blocks your path to the future and its shadow looms over everything you do. Seen in this light, a mountain could be any number of seemingly invincible obstacles: life-threatening illness, relentless opposition, lack of finance, to name just a few. How are we to respond to such large and seemingly immovable problems? Jesus tells us to confront these difficult situations with the certain confidence that nothing is too hard for the Lord. Instead of telling God how big your problem is, Jesus urges you to tell the mountain how big your God is! Speak to your mountain with unshakable certainty. Tell the mountain, "You may be great but my God is greater!" Sooner or later, that thing is going to shift and move. The word "impossible" is not in heaven's dictionary!

Creativity

"I've personally chosen Bezalel son of
Uri, son of Hur of the tribe of Judah.
I've filled him with the Spirit of God,
giving him skill and know-how and
expertise in every kind of craft to create
designs and work in gold, silver, and
bronze; to cut and set gemstones; to carve
wood—he's an all-around craftsman."

Exodus 31:1–5

Have you ever gone to your Heavenly Father and asked Him to give you creativity for a particular project? One of the things we need to remember is that we are all made in the image of the Maker. That means that we are all creative because God is creative. Sometimes we make the mistake of telling ourselves that we are not creative, perhaps because that is a lie we were made to believe early on in our lives. At other times we may make the mistake of thinking that God only wants to fill us with His Spirit for traditional forms of ministry in His church, like preaching. But Bezalel was empowered by the Holy Spirit to provide heavenly designs for the interior of the Tabernacle of Moses—in other words, for an artistic project! Ask God to equip you with the heavenly ideas, patterns, equations, blueprints, designs, stories, poems, songs and other things you need. He's extraordinarily creative. He wants to help you to be creative too.

Deliverance

"I will rescue you from slavery."

EXODUS 6:6

To be enslaved to a substance, lifestyle, or way of thinking is a dreadful torment. We not only find ourselves controlled and enslaved, we bring others whom we love into that slavery too. When that happens, and we see the pain our addictions cause, a cry begins to emerge from our hearts, "O God, deliver me!" This heartfelt prayer is the beginning of our liberation. Only when we yield our bound-up hearts to our kind and gracious Savior will freedom start to come to us and to our co-dependent loved ones. If you are oppressed and feel enslaved, ask Jesus to help you. Jesus is your Strong Deliverer, your Chain-Breaker! Let Him be your Lord, not just your Friend. When you renounce your addiction and let Jesus rule over your life, He promises that He will rescue, shield and protect you from the deadly hazards of the enemy.

Desire

*You can be sure that God will take
care of everything you need.*
PHILIPPIANS 4:19

How can we be sure that God will meet our greatest needs and fulfill our deepest desires? The key here is to put Him first in our lives and to take a greater delight in Him than in anything or anyone else in our world. When our greatest pleasure is to worship Him, to commune with Him, to seek and do His will, then our desires will align with His desires. When this occurs, then it becomes so much easier to know and trust that He will take care of everything we need. This is precisely what King David learned. He learned that when a person starts to delight in the Lord, then the Lord will fulfill the desires of their heart (Psalm 37:4). When we hope for things that are outside of His will, our hearts become sick. But when we desire the things He desires, then we find ourselves living life in all its fullness (Proverbs 13:12). Make it your aim to align your desires with His, and then see Him work to fulfill every one of them in time.

Employment

"If God gives such attention to the appearance of wildflowers—most of which are never even seen—don't you think he'll attend to you, take pride in you, do his best for you?"

MATTHEW 6:30

When we find ourselves out of work, we can sometimes experience a severe loss of confidence. We have been in employment and earned enough to provide for ourselves and maybe others too. We have had tasks to complete and this has given us a measure of purpose. We have received a salary and this has helped to pay our rent or mortgage and even to have some down time with family and friends. Now that's gone and we ask, "Where is God in this?" The answer is that He's right with you, encouraging you to trust Him. He gives amazing attention to the welfare of everything in His creation, including wildflowers! You are of far greater value than they. You are His pride and joy! If you seek Him first, He'll meet your needs. All you have to do is put first things first and then watch as He opens new doors that none can shut!

Encouragement

*When you're in over your head, I'll be there
with you. When you're in rough waters, you
will not go down. When you're between a
rock and a hard place, it won't be a dead
end—Because I am God, your personal
God, The Holy of Israel, your Savior.*

Isaiah 43:2

If ever there was a word of encouragement from heaven it is this. Maybe you are going through a really rough time in your life right now. Perhaps you have to go through major surgery or you are facing the prospect of redundancy. Perhaps you are facing a trial or you are going through a painful divorce. Isn't it encouraging that at these times God is not far away but very near? Isn't it a comfort to know that our Heavenly Father is not aloof from our sufferings but that He is Immanuel, God with us in our testing circumstances? If you're in a situation where you're in over your head, or sailing through rough waters, or stuck between a rock and a hard place, be encouraged. God is with you. Your Father is right there by your side. He'll keep your head above water. He'll bring you out of stormy seas into calmer straits. He'll not let you go down a hard road only to find that it's a dead end. He's your personal God and Savior. He is infinitely fond of you. He wants the best for you. He will guide you through. The best years lie ahead.

Energy

He energizes those who get tired,
gives fresh strength to dropouts.
For even young people tire and drop out,
young folk in their prime stumble and fall.
But those who wait upon God get fresh
strength. They spread their wings and
soar like eagles, They run and don't get
tired, they walk and don't lag behind.
ISAIAH 40:29–31

From time to time we can be overwhelmed by a loss of energy. This can be due to doing too much at work or in ministry and failing to take proper rest. It can be due to mental exhaustion, brought on by grief or shame, despair or discouragement. It can be due to moral failure and the consequent disconnection from the one who cannot look upon sin and yet who longs to give us all that we need when we turn our faces back to Him. Whatever the reason, God our Heavenly Father is waiting. When we turn from looking down to looking up, from depending upon ourselves to relying upon Him, He energizes us in spirit, soul and body. He gives us the motivation to spread our wings again and He lifts us up. If you need energy today, ask God to fill you with His life-giving Spirit. Let His strength arise in your weakness so that you can run again and not grow tired.

Faith

> *"I believe. Help me with my doubts!"*
> MARK 9:24

Have you ever been in this situation? You believe intellectually. You give assent in your mind to the truth that Jesus is the Son of God and that He is the Savior and Healer. But in the face of a specific challenge—a chronic sickness or a desperate job situation—you experience doubts in your heart. You cannot believe that God will answer your prayer and meet your need. In Mark 9, a father brings his boy to Jesus. His son is oppressed by demons and subject to dangerous seizures. He tells Jesus, "If you can do anything, do it!" Jesus then tells him, "There are no 'ifs' among believers." The father then asks Jesus to help him with his doubts. Jesus answers by setting the boy free. Maybe you are facing a specific challenge right now. Get rid of your "ifs." Ask Jesus to give you the gift of faith. Trust Him to reveal that He is not only alive but All-Powerful. Trust Him to do something doubt-destroying in your life!

Family

> Your wife will bear children as a vine
> bears grapes, your household lush as a
> vineyard, The children around your table
> as fresh and promising as young olive
> shoots. Stand in awe of God's Yes. Oh,
> how he blesses the one who fears God!
>
> PSALM 128:3–4

God loves family because He is Himself a family—a family of three persons, Father, Son and Holy Spirit. It should therefore come as no surprise that He wants to bless our families. This we should make a regular practice. If we cannot speak a blessing over them face to face, then we can speak it over them in the secret place where we pray to the Father. If your family is in trouble right now, if it is divided or oppressed, ask the Father to restore His divine order to your family life. Speak the blessings of Psalm 128 over it. Make sure that you pray with the heart of "one who fears the Lord." This holy fear is not the toxic terror of God's punishment. It is a healthy reverence for God's greatness, holiness and radiance. Pray with this deep-seated awe and respect for the majesty of God. It is this that will fuel your prayers and will cause marriages to be fruitful, households to be plentiful, and children to be purposeful, fulfilling the promises of God over their lives. If your family has needs right now, renew your devotion and increase your intercession. The God who is three-in-one, the eternal family, will come through for you.

Filling

"Don't you think the Father who conceived you in love will give the Holy Spirit when you ask him?"

LUKE 11:13

Have you ever felt spiritually empty? You feel as if you're running on empty and you can't go on any more. The temptation in these sorts of seasons is either to hide away, as if we were the only person who ever felt this way, or to give up. But neither isolation nor desolation is the answer. We need to recognize that the most significant moments of our lives are often when we are at the end of our rope. When we arrive at the end of our own resources, we find the beginning of His. God delights in filling empty vessels. He loves to pour His Spirit into those who have poured themselves out on Him and on others. Indeed, self-emptying is the pathway to being Spirit-filled. If you feel empty today, come to God as a trusting child before your generous Father. Know with certainty that He loves you so much that He will fill lavish you with the power of His Holy Spirit, filling the empty spaces of your life with His amazing love.

Focus

I've got my eye on the goal, where God is beckoning us onward—to Jesus. I'm off and running, and I'm not turning back. So let's keep focused on that goal.

PHILIPPIANS 3:14–15

The Apostle Paul compares his life to a marathon race. He tells his readers that he's got one goal: he's not going to look back or turn round. He's not going to give up. He's going to press on towards the prize that Jesus has in store for those who finish well. This is Paul's priority, which is why he says, "Let's keep focused." Every one of us needs a focus in life. We need to be able to say with Paul, "One thing I do." At a general level, every believer needs to have the same focus which is to finish well. At the same time we are also called to a particular mission in life. Ask the Father today to give you greater focus. He wants you to know what He's put you on this earth to do. He wants you to know that you're here by appointment, not by accident. Lay down your "day-dream" and take up your "God-dream." When you do, you'll be able to say, "I've got my eye on the goal."

Forgiveness

You're well-known as good and forgiving,
bighearted to all who ask for help.
Pay attention, God, to my prayer;
bend down and listen to my cry for help.

PSALM 86:5–6

A very famous pop singer was interviewed not long ago for his biography. After three hundred pages of answering one question after another about his life and music he was asked one final question. "Is there anything that makes you speechless?" That was a good question; the man was renowned for speaking, and particularly for seemingly never stopping! The celebrity paused for a moment before answering. Then he replied. "Forgiveness…especially being forgiven." If there's one thing that should make us all speechless it's being forgiven. Forgiveness is a gift we don't deserve. The good news is that we have a Heavenly Father who is bighearted, full of mercy, and abounding in compassion. He is well-known throughout the earth for being a kind Father who loves to forgive His children. If you need forgiveness today, position yourself before your Father as a child. Ask Him to hear your cry, "I'm sorry." Watch as He bends down to embrace and forgive you. Let it make you speechless too.

Gladness

God anointed me...To care for the needs
of all who mourn in Zion, give them
bouquets of roses instead of ashes, Messages
of joy instead of news of doom, a praising
heart instead of a languid spirit.

ISAIAH 61:1–3

There are times in many peoples' lives, including the lives of those who know and trust God, when all we seem to be able to experience is a great sadness. Maybe we are struck down with grief at the passing of a loved one. Maybe we are weighed down by self-doubt as the result of a loss of position or purpose. Maybe we are confused and troubled in our minds and hearts and we just don't know where to turn for help or when it will ever end. When such seasons come, where can we turn? While some may need to look to medication, all of us can look to the Messiah. He gives roses to those who are ashen with grief. He gives good news to those disturbed by bad news. He exchanges our languid spirits for praising hearts. If you are wearing a garment of despair today, let Jesus remove it and clothe you with a mantle of praise. He is the one who anoints our troubled minds with the oil of gladness and turns our depression into dancing.

Guidance

Your teacher will be right there, local and on the job, urging you on whenever you wander left or right: "This is the right road. Walk down this road."
ISAIAH 30:21

We all have a teacher with us at all times. That teacher is called the Holy Spirit. He is the one who gives us instruction about the ways and the purposes of God. If you are in need of guidance, ask the Holy Spirit to teach you to see the path you're meant to travel. Ask Him to let you know that "this is the right road." Sometimes we have very tough decisions to make in life. How can we know we have received God's guidance? Employ the STARS test. S stands for Scripture: Is this decision a biblical one? T stands for Testimony: What witness do you have in your heart that this course of action is the right one? A is for Advice: What counsel have you been given by older and wiser Christians? R stands for Revelation: Have you received guidance in the form of a vision or a dream, as our ancestors in the Bible did? S stands for Situation: Is there anything in your circumstances that indicates that this is the right time and the right direction for you? When we have big decisions about direction, the Holy Spirit is our teacher. He is our internal satellite navigation system. Let's follow His lead.

Healing

"*I'll doctor the injured, I'll build up
the weak ones and oversee the strong
ones so they're not exploited.*"
EZEKIEL 34:16

In Ezekiel 34, God expresses His anger towards the shepherds of Israel—those called to be pastors of His people, the spiritual guardians of His flock. He rebukes these men for being bad shepherds, for exploiting their position and abusing their people. He then tells His people that even though these pastors were called to represent His love, they have failed badly. God then likens Himself to a Good Shepherd and promises that He will heal those who have been wounded, strengthen those who are weak, and watch over His people to ensure that in the future they are not oppressed. See here the Father's love and compassion for those who are physically, emotionally and spiritually wounded. Take heart today. Jesus is the Great Physician. He brings healing to those who are oppressed and depressed, sick and weak. Our God is a God of healing. If you need to be restored to health in body, mind, soul and spirit, come to the Good Shepherd. It won't be long before help arrives from heaven.

Hope

> *"I know what I'm doing. I have it all planned out—plans to take care of you, not abandon you, plans to give you the future you hope for."*
> **JEREMIAH 29:11**

What a great thing it is to know that we have a Father who has a dream for our lives—a dream to give us a hopeful future and to prosper us, not to harm us. Every person in the world needs hope. This is one of three things that human beings need most—forgiveness for the past, a meaningful life in the present, and a hope for the future. At times it can be hard to be hopeful. We may be knee-deep in children's laundry or endlessly filing other people's paperwork and we may find it hard to think of ourselves as anything other than hamsters going round and round in an endless, monotonous wheel in a large and gloomy cage. But this is not going to be the whole story. Most of us go through phases where our profession and our passion don't line up. In those seasons we need to trust the Father that our work is not in vain and that one day preparation will meet opportunity. If you are a Christian, trust God that His dream for your life will unfold and that His purposes will be fulfilled. Keep on hoping, believing that you will experience a glorious convergence of what you do and what makes you feel most alive!

Increase

> *"Clear lots of ground for your tents!*
> *Make your tents large. Spread*
> *out! Think big! Use plenty of rope,*
> *drive the tent pegs deep."*
> ISAIAH 54:2–3

When Jesus was 12 years old, He became separated from His parents in Jerusalem. When they eventually relocated Him, they were understandably upset. Jesus however replied, "Didn't you know I had to be about my Father's business?" There are two types of business we can be about. We can be about our own or we can be about our Father's. Whose business are you about? If you are about the Father's business then increase is already built into the heavenly blueprints of what you're doing. The kingdom of heaven is not about decline and death. It is about expansion and life. If you're about the Father's business, then ask God to move you from the day of small things to the day of greater things. Ask Him to give you dynamic expansion as you prove yourself faithful to Him when you have little. He will sooner or later call to you from heaven, tell you to think big and give you the signal to enlarge the place of your tent. Then you will see increase all around you.

Influence

God will make you the head, not
the tail; you'll always be the top
dog, never the bottom dog, as you
obediently listen to and diligently keep
the commands of God, your God.
DEUTERONOMY 28:13

It can be an infuriating and soul-destroying thing to find you are always being led and never have a chance to lead. If that's you, take heart. The Father wants you to discover one of the rewards for those who respond obediently to His Word. Those who consistently hear and obey God are in for some serious blessings! One of these is that we will cease being the bottom dog in our place of work or our circles of ministry. Those who put God first will find that they are not always last in line and under everyone else's authority. Their sphere of influence will gradually increase. As they prove faithful and trustworthy with a small amount of influence, so they will be given greater and greater amounts. In this way, whatever their circle of ministry or work, they will find that their faithfulness is rewarded with continuous graduation and promotion. Instead of always being the tail, they will be the head. If you are looking for influence, work on your personal obedience to the commands of God. As you do, your integrity will become more visible and the reward will be more influence.

Joy

*Oh! May the God of green
hope fill you up with joy!*
ROMANS 15:13

Joy is one of the hallmarks of those who love Jesus. It is something far deeper than what the world understands by joy. To the unbeliever, joy is a feeling of happiness that is almost always and entirely dependent on beneficial and pleasurable circumstances. When a person achieves success at work or in the sports arena, they are joyful. When a person gets married they are overjoyed. Joy in the world's eyes is entirely related to positive circumstances. Not so for the Christian. For the follower of Jesus, joy is something that the Holy Spirit grows in us over time, irrespective of our circumstances. Joy is an internal capacity to be elated and hopeful even when our outward circumstances are far from positive. Joy in all circumstances, especially in adversity, is a hallmark of the Christian life. When the believer is bereaved or afflicted, they still find a way to rejoice. This is something that both astounds and confounds our non-Christian friends. Only God could do that. So may the God of green hope fill you to overflowing with joy!

Justice

> *He won't yell, won't raise his voice;*
> *there'll be no commotion in the streets.*
> *He won't walk over anyone's feelings,*
> *won't push you into a corner.*
>
> MATTHEW 12:20

Have you ever been a victim of injustice? Have you ever been badly wronged? Do you stand in need of vindication? Do you need someone to exonerate and liberate you? If so, be encouraged. You have a champion, a spokesman, a mighty activist and perfect judge. Jesus is the Servant of the Lord who brings healing to those who are victims of injustice in the nations. He does this by behaving in the opposite spirit to those who oppress the powerless. He does not rage and shout. He does not treat people like doormats, walking all over them. He doesn't abuse power and position to make others feel cornered or trapped. No, as Matthew reports in this verse, Jesus is altogether different. He is gentle with those who are bruised and battered. He is sensitive and compassionate to those whose lives have almost been extinguished. Come to Jesus if you need His justice. He is the voice for those who have no voice, the Word for those whose words aren't heard.

Kindness

> *"You were extravagantly generous in love with David my father, and he lived faithfully in your presence, his relationships were just and his heart right. And you have persisted in this great and generous love."*
> 1 KINGS 3:6

God is a specialist in kindness, or in what Solomon here calls "great and generous love." Kindness is one of the most beautiful virtues. Kindness can be defined as the act of showing someone gentle consideration and generous love when they are too poor or lost to do anything for themselves. It can be understood as an attitude of heart that accepts and honors others even when they are in a mess, sometimes of their own making. Seen in that light, God truly is kind. He continually turns His face towards us and shows us love that we haven't deserved and do not deserve. He constantly honors us even when we have wandered far from Him and, like the prodigal son, come home with nothing but our shame. God is the kindest Father in the universe. He continued to show kindness to King David, Solomon's father, even though he made mistakes. He continues to show kindness to us too. Pray for more of this kindness today. It is the most life-changing quality in the universe (Romans 2:4).

Love

> *First we were loved, now we love. He loved us first.*
> **1 JOHN 4:19**

The two greatest needs we have are to love and to be loved. There are no needs greater than these. However, it is far easier to give love if you have first received it. Receiving love increases our capacity to give it. This is why the Apostle John, when he comes to teach us all about loving one another in the family of God, makes sure we realize that we were loved first. Before we ever loved God or our neighbor, God loved us first. That is a great mystery and a great marvel! The great God, who has the universe to rule, has stepped down into our world and demonstrated His love for each and every one of us. He did this supremely in the sending of His Son, Jesus Christ, who died in our place at Calvary. If you want to know what love is, look at the Cross. If you want to receive that love, go to the Cross where the Savior's arms are open wide. See the lavish and outrageous love of God! He has loved you to death and He has loved you to hell and back. Let this love saturate your soul. Receive it today. Know that He first loved you. Then give that love away to others. It's too good to keep to yourself!

Marriage

God said, "It's not good for the Man to be
alone; I'll make him a helper, a companion."
GENESIS 2:18

Loneliness afflicts countless people in every country and on every continent. Loneliness is not necessarily the state of being physically on your own. It is not having someone with whom you can share your heart on a day-to-day basis. Tragically, this is true both inside and outside the church. There are many people who long for deeper friendships, for love, for marriage. What is a person to do in this situation? There are no straightforward or simple solutions, but one thing we can do is remind our loving, Heavenly Father of what He wrote into the foundations of creation—that it is not a good and healthy thing for a human being to be alone. It is harmful for us not to have someone in our lives with whom we can share our hearts. Then we can ask Him to do again what He did in Eden—to give us a helper and companion, someone with whom we can travel on the journey of life, someone with whom we can be entirely comfortable and with whom we can have unity in heart, mind, soul and strength.

Miracles

Jesus doesn't change—yesterday, today, tomorrow, he's always totally himself.

HEBREWS 13:8

Do you need a miracle today? Do you need Jesus to set you free from some dreadful affliction from the enemy? Do you need Him to heal you of some illness or other? Do you need Him to multiply what little you have and make it go further than it ever could without His intervention? Do you need Him to give you heaven's peace in an earthly storm? Do you need His miraculous provision in a time of lack? If so, remember what Jesus did two thousand years ago. He healed the sick, cleansed the lepers, gave sight to the blind, raised the dead, provided for the hungry, brought peace to the storm-struck, delivered the demonized and gave dignity to the vilified. Has our Jesus changed since then? No, not one little bit. Jesus Christ is the same yesterday, today and forever! He's always the same. He's always totally Himself. Miracles are not something He did then but doesn't do now! No, God says, "I am your Healer," not, "I was your Healer" (Exodus 15:26). Put your trust in Jesus. Ask Him to stretch out His mighty hand and bless your life or your loved ones' lives with His life-changing power.

Money

> I once was young, now I'm a graybeard—
> not once have I seen an abandoned
> believer, or his kids out roaming the streets.
> Every day he's out giving and lending,
> his children making him proud.
> PSALM 37:25–26

There are times in most of our lives when we are financially challenged, when we are concerned how bills are going to be paid and food put on the table for our loved ones. When these seasons comes it is so tempting to let go of our faith in God's all-sufficient provision and to forget His faithfulness to us in the past. What we need in these situations is a good, strong reminder that God is a loving, perfect Father who never abandons His children and who never allows us to be so impoverished that our kids have to go out onto the streets. The writer of Psalm 37 says, "I'm a very old man with gray hair but I've never seen God forsake the righteous or their offspring resort to begging for bread…no, not once!" If we continue to live in a right relationship with God (which is part of what the word "righteous" means), then we can be absolutely sure that we will not see it either! He will provide for all our needs. More than that, we will have enough to give and lend with the same generosity that we have received.

Nourishment

> *"Why do you spend your money on junk food, your hard-earned cash on cotton candy? Listen to me, listen well: Eat only the best, fill yourself with only the finest."*
>
> ISAIAH 55:3–4

Do you feel weary and worn out? Do you feel as if you've been giving out all the time? Do you feel spiritually broke and emotionally famished? If so, it's time to retreat, rest and recharge your batteries. Don't look to what the world has to offer to fill your empty spaces. God has something far more satisfying in store for you. He has resources in heaven that He longs for you to enjoy on earth, especially His mighty power and amazing love. Everything you need to turn your hunger into fullness is accessed through feeding on God's Word and living according to His ways. When you bring yourself into realignment with the timeless wisdom of the Word of God, you position yourself for favor and fullness. So feast on what is most fulfilling—the nourishing words of God in the Bible. Let the Father's truths fill your tired life. Let His Spirit fill your thirsty soul. What the world has to offer you is junk food. What the Father offers is a royal banquet.

Opportunity

> "I see what you've done. Now see what
> I've done. I've opened a door before
> you that no one can slam shut."
>
> **REVELATION 3:8**

Are you looking for a new season in your life, a time of fresh beginnings and new opportunities? Sometimes we get the distinct impression that the door is closing onto an old way of doing things, a familiar job or ministry. We sense that transition is in the air and that God is calling us to move on into pastures new. When this happens there is an understandable temptation to push doors, to investigate and apply for new opportunities. While there is a lot to be said for initiative-taking, we must make sure that it is God's initiative we are pursuing, not our own, God's dream we are following, not our daydream. When we push doors in our own strength we often become exhausted and dispirited. When we let go and let God take control, then instead of putting our shoulder to many doors, one door swings open. When that happens Jesus says, "I've seen your efforts. Now look at mine!" The critical thing is to let Jesus be sovereign in all of this. He is the King of Kings. Let Him open the door. And when He does, remember the old saying: "The opportunity of a lifetime needs to be seized in the lifetime of an opportunity."

Peace

> *"I'm leaving you well and whole. That's my parting gift to you. Peace."*
> **JOHN 14:26**

Are you experiencing anxiety in your life right now? If so, trust in this wonderful promise that Jesus gave to His disciples the night before He died. This is something they were going to need. Within 24 hours their Master and Friend would be dead. They would be terribly afraid. They would need that heavenly peace that the world cannot provide. We need it too. Our course is not always through calm and storm-free waters. When turbulence comes, we need the peace of the Lord on the inside so that we can remain secure even while the world outside is being shaken. The good news is that Jesus promises His peace to us too. The word "peace" is a beautiful, all-encompassing idea in the Bible. It refers to peace at every level—peace with God, peace with others, peace within, and peace with our world. When Jesus promises His peace, He is referring not only to inner serenity but wholeness in all our dealings, all our relationships. Claim this promise. Tell Jesus, "I believe it. Now I receive it."

Perseverance

We pray that you'll have the strength to stick it out over the long haul—not the grim strength of gritting your teeth but the glory-strength God gives. It is strength that endures the unendurable and spills over into joy.

COLOSSIANS 1:10–11

When we give our lives to Christ, an epic journey begins in which there are many high points where our mouths are filled with laughter and many valleys in which our eyes are filled with tears. Becoming a Christian does not mean that we will "live happily after." That is a fairy tale. No, the Christian life is a life of many challenges and hardships as well as many miracles and breakthroughs. We therefore need to set our sails for the long haul and understand that our lives will not always be plain sailing. There will be storms in which the waves are high and the wind strong. This is why we need to have a persevering heart, a heart that says, "I will never quit. I will not be a fair-weather Christian. I will commit myself to the long haul, whatever storms may come." The good news is that God promises He will give us heavenly power in this journey—not the endurance of gritted teeth but the glory-strength of heaven. This gives us joy even in our sufferings and helps us to endure the unendurable. Pray to God for His glory-strength today.

Presence

*If your heart is broken, you'll
find God right there.*
PSALM 34:18

Corrie ten Boom and her sister Betsie were Dutch Christians. During the Second World War, they and their family were arrested and then sent to a concentration camp for harboring and helping Jewish fugitives. While they were incarcerated, Betsie became sick and died. Before she went to glory, she told Corrie to tell the world that "there is no pit of suffering so deep that Jesus is not deeper still." What did Betsie mean? She meant that Jesus is not aloof from our pain or beyond suffering, like the gods of other philosophies and religions. No, Jesus has entered into the worst of our suffering. He has experienced life as a fugitive, an exile and a victim of great injustice. He has suffered what we suffer and He understands. Whatever pit of pain we enter, He is deeper still. If your heart is broken today and you need comfort, know that God Himself is with you, drying your tears, holding you close, saying, "I am with you."

Prosperity

"Bless me, O bless me! Give me land, large tracts of land. And provide your personal protection—don't let evil hurt me."

1 Chronicles 4:10

If the prayer of Jesus—known as the Lord's Prayer—is the model prayer in the New Testament, the prayer of Jabez is the model prayer in the Old. Here a man called Jabez—from the tribe of Judah—is described as a better man than his brothers, a man of honor. God is clearly especially fond of him for that reason. He is also especially fond of him because of the way he prays. He shows complete trust in his Heavenly Father for two things—the enlargement of his territory and protection from evil. God grants him both requests. Is it wrong for us to pray the same? Not if God has a plan to *prosper* and not to harm us (Jeremiah 29:11). Ask God for the blessing of His prosperity. Ask Him twice, as Jabez does: "Bless me, O bless me!" When we live under the Father's blessing, we are given increase and enlargement in the sphere of our influence and we are granted personal protection against the pain the enemy wants to cause us. So be a person of honor. Your honor is the pathway to God's favor.

Protection

Say this: "God, you're my refuge.
I trust in you and I'm safe!"
That's right—he rescues you from hidden
traps, shields you from deadly hazards.
His huge outstretched arms protect you—
under them you're perfectly safe."

PSALM 91:2–4

Those who live as faithful sons and daughters of God will always know His heavenly protection. Obedience to our Heavenly Father brings so many rewards, not least the ongoing assurance of His safety. When we are disobedient, the Father has to look away from us because He cannot stand to look on sin. He withdraws His protective blessing from us until we return to Him again. The lesson is clear: when we are faithful, He keeps us under the shelter of His protective love. To be faithful is therefore the key. So what does it mean to be faithful? It means simply to be full of faith. Faith means trusting that what you cannot yet see is real. When we believe God even while we cannot see Him, that is faith. When we say, "God, you're my refuge even though I cannot see your outstretched arms," that is faith. When we walk by faith and not by sight, God protects us from the hidden traps and the deadly hazards that the enemy assigns for us. Underneath the mighty arms of God, we are always secure and perfectly safe.

Quietness

You have bedded me down in lush meadows, you find me quiet pools to drink from. True to your word, you let me catch my breath and send me in the right direction.

PSALM 23:2–3

We are all wired differently, but one thing we all need from time to time is a place of peace and quiet where we can rest "far from the madding crowd." If we don't find these oases in the midst of noise and hurry, we feel aggravated, robbed and flustered. This is especially true if we get a sense that God is trying to speak to us, maybe about a new direction or a fresh way of seeing things, and we are simply too busy to stop long enough to hear His voice. When that happens it is especially frustrating. Two things are then most likely to happen in this situation. The first is that we become intentional about finding "quiet pools." We take the initiative and discipline ourselves to find and maximize the space and time to be quiet before the Lord. The second is that the Lord "makes us lie down." He creates a circumstance where we have to rest and have to listen. The first is always preferable. So ask your Heavenly Father to lead you to those quiet pools where you can catch your breath and receive His new directions for your life.

Rescue

*"In trouble, deep trouble, I prayed to God.
He answered me. From the belly of the
grave I cried, 'Help!' You heard my cry."*

JONAH 2:1

There are three kinds of storms. There are first of all storms that God uses to bring us back to obedience. This is the kind that Jonah experiences. Then there is secondly the kind of storm that the devil sends to destroy us. This is the kind that Jesus experiences in Mark 4. The third is the kind that the Roman centurion Julius experiences in Acts 27. This is neither heaven-sent nor hell-sent. It is simply part and parcel of living in a fallen world. If you're going through a storm right now, determine what kind it is. If it's sent from God, repent and get back on track as Jonah did as he turned to God in the belly of the whale. If it's sent from the devil, rebuke it. If it's neither, then do what Paul encouraged Julius to do—rest until it passes! Whatever the storm, God wants to rescue us, but the pathway to that rescue will depend upon us discerning the right source of the storm and then deciding on the right strategy.

Reconciliation

> *"He will convince parents to look after their children and children to look up to their parents."*
> **MALACHI 4:6**

The closing words of the Old Testament contain a great promise—that one day God will send someone into the world that will turn the hearts of the fathers towards their children and the hearts of the children towards their parents. That someone was of course Jesus, who alone can save and heal divided families. Today there are many families throughout the world in which parents have become estranged from their children, and children from their parents. There are many prodigal sons and daughters who have left their parents. There are many prodigal fathers and mothers who have left their children. If your need is for reconciliation between parent and child, if your need is for a restoration of healthy, loving relationships between children and their parents, claim this promise as you pray. Ask your Heavenly Father, who knows what it is to have children reject Him, to give you faith for reconciliation. Ask Jesus to bring relational healing. There is no one better at reconciliation.

Rest

"Are you tired? Worn out? Burned out
on religion? Come to me. Get away
with me and you'll recover your life.
I'll show you how to take a real rest."

MATTHEW 11:28

Jesus here promises rest when we are weary. What kind of weariness is He talking about here? He is talking about the exhaustion of religious striving. Jesus did not come to start a religion. He came to start a relationship. Religion places great expectations upon us. It tells us that we will never be accepted by God unless we measure up to countless rules and regulations. Religion is accordingly a performance-based system. It creates a culture where everyone tries to earn God's approval by doing good works. What Jesus offers is totally different. He teaches that God is not a demanding slave-master who demands we earn His acceptance but a loving Father who invites us to know His acceptance by simply trusting in His Son. When we do that, we exchange the heavy burden of religion for the light burden of relationship—a relationship that brings us rest. No longer do we work for God's approval. We work from His approval because we know that in Jesus we are accepted and loved. This is the place of rest and it is a place of grace, not law.

Restoration

Heart-shattered lives ready for love
don't for a moment escape God's notice.

PSALM 51:17

This wonderful truth is found in a song that David composed after he had sinned (Psalm 51). He had committed adultery and murder and in the process broken two of the Ten Commandments. That by any standards was a grave moral failure. David was utterly crushed when he eventually came to his senses. Having had his conscience pricked through the rebuke of the prophet Nathan, he repented of his sins with godly sorrow and turned his face towards his loving Father in heaven. He presented himself before God as a heart-shattered life. He told the Father that his heart was ready to receive love—not the earthly love of a human being but the divine love that alone can ultimately satisfy the soul. With that the restoration began. Whenever we come before God with broken hearts, we can rest assured that we won't for a moment escape the Father's loving gaze. When we break up, He breaks in. When we break down, He breaks through. He will never despise a broken heart. While religious people may disqualify us, our loving Father doesn't.

Resurrection

Since Jesus died and broke loose from the grave, God will most certainly bring back to life those who died in Jesus.

1 THESSALONIANS 4:14

When a loved one dies, it leaves a gaping, gnawing hole in our hearts. The Apostle Paul knew full well that the agonizing experience of bereavement is one that all of us will have to endure at one time or another, which is why, at the end of First Thessalonians 4, he seeks to encourage us with one single, beautiful thought: for the Christian, death is not a hopeless end but rather an endless hope. For the Christian, death is the gateway to a glorious new existence. How was Paul so certain? The answer is simple. He had met the risen Jesus! He knew as a fact that Jesus had been dead but was now alive forever. Paul reasoned that if that had happened to Jesus, then it would happen to those who invite Jesus into their hearts. This stands to reason. If the One who conquered death lives within us, then what happened to Him will surely happen to us! We will one day be raised from death with brand new, glorious, imperishable, resurrection bodies. So take heart. Those who die in Jesus get to live forever!

Salvation

God...got us out of the mess we're in and
restored us to where he always wanted us to
be. And he did it by means of Jesus Christ.
ROMANS 3:24

The Bible teaches that we all need rescuing. We are all of us in the wrong in God's eyes because of our sin—our refusal to put God first. We stand condemned to spiritual death, to a life and eternity separated from our loving Heavenly Father. We are therefore in a terrible mess. But the good news is that God loved us far too much to leave us there. He sent Jesus into the world to get us out of the mess we were in and into the place He always wanted us to be. Thanks to Jesus, salvation is now possible. All you have to do is confess your sin and believe that Jesus paid the penalty and God will put things right. More than that, when you ask Jesus into your heart you receive His righteousness—His right standing before God. That is glorious news! It means that while once you were in the wrong, now you are in the right, all because of Jesus Christ!

Serenity

Don't fret or worry. Instead of worrying, pray. Let petitions and praises shape your worries into prayers, letting God know your concerns. Before you know it, a sense of God's wholeness, everything coming together for good, will come and settle you down. It's wonderful what happens when Christ displaces worry at the center of your life.

PHILIPPIANS 4:6–7

There are really two sorts of people in the church: those who live from a center of fear and those who live from a center of love. Those who live from a center of fear are like spiritual orphans. They live with a permanent anxiety. They worry about whether they are good enough and whether others approve of them. They worry about whether there is ever going to be enough money in the bank or food on the table. They live with a fear about everything and they are even afraid that God won't accept them. Those who live from a love center are the exact opposite. They are like sons and daughters. They know that they are greatly loved. They work from approval not for approval. They trust in their Heavenly Father for all their financial and practical needs, never doubting that their needs will be met. If you have worries, respond like a son or a daughter, not like an orphan. Turn your worry into worship and let the perfect love of Jesus displace the anxiety and fear at the center of your lives.

Strength

> *"My grace is enough; it's all you need. My strength comes into its own in your weakness."*
>
> 2 CORINTHIANS 12:9

One of our most human tendencies is trying to do everything in our own strength. We rely on our own resources to get things done and to achieve success. The trouble with this is that the Bible calls this sin. Sin is our endless capacity to try and manage our entire lives on our own, in our own strength. This is not the path to breakthrough. Sin says, "I'll make it on my own," and in saying that immediately undermines the possibility of receiving an invasion of God's grace. God's grace, His energizing and empowering strength, comes to those who do not rely on themselves and who have renounced the idol of self-sufficiency. Grace breaks through into the lives of those who come to the end of themselves, who feel so weak they know that any breakthrough that might come from here on would have to be God. This is the place that the Apostle Paul inhabited—a place of utter dependency on God's power. When we are weakest, God is strongest. Ask for the strength of God's grace to do what He has called you to do. "It's all you need."

Truth

"I will talk to the Father, and he'll provide you another Friend so that you will always have someone with you. This Friend is the Spirit of Truth."

JOHN 14:16

Pontius Pilate, faced with the challenge of finding out whether Jesus was innocent or guilty, asked, "What is truth?" The irony of course is that Jesus had already told His disciples, "I am the Truth." Truth, in other words, is not a philosophy to be understood or a principle to be discovered. It is a person to be known. Once a person commits to knowing Jesus, they commit to knowing the Truth. Jesus is the Truth and He is the Truth about everything. If you and I want to discover the truth about any subject under the sun, then the closer we are to Jesus, the closer we will find ourselves to the Truth. This involves renouncing the lie that says we can know the truth through the use of our natural minds. No, we need the Holy Spirit. He is the Spirit of Truth and He is our Friend! If you need to understand the truth about anything, lean on Jesus and ask your Friend, the Holy Spirit. God has promised that He will give us spiritual minds that can understand spiritual truths.

Unction

> *Christ's anointing teaches you the truth on everything you need to know about yourself and him, uncontaminated by a single lie.*
>
> 1 JOHN 2:27

The word unction means "anointing." The Bible teaches us that Jesus Christ was the Anointed One. That is the literal meaning of the word Hebrew word "Messiah" and its Greek translation "Christ." Christ means "Anointed One." Jesus said in His first ever sermon that the Spirit of the Lord was upon Him and that He had been anointed to bring Good News to the poor. If Jesus Christ was anointed for the task of telling the truth about God, then how much more should we be! This is where the verse from 1 John 2 is such an encouragement. The Bible tells us that we are all of us "anointed ones" if we are Christians. The anointing of God's Holy Spirit rests upon us and gives us the ability to distinguish truth from error and to speak the truth to others. This has huge implications. Don't pray for the anointing as if you don't already have it! Pray for more of what you already have—the unction that makes you like Jesus and gives you access to the truth on everything you need to know about who you are and who He is!

Victory

No test or temptation that comes your way is beyond the course of what others have had to face. All you need to remember is that God will never let you down; he'll never let you be pushed past your limit; he'll always be there to help you come through it.

1 CORINTHIANS 10:13

There are times in every Christian's life when the enemy attacks us with temptation after temptation. Perhaps it comes at a time when we are exhausted and low, when our defenses are down and we are particularly vulnerable. When we are in this condition, we are particularly open to spiritual attack. This attack can come in any number of forms: a consistent assault on our integrity from intimidating people; an act of great injustice against us; a continuous and seductive enticement to give in to money, sex and power. The scenarios are numerous. That's the bad news. But the good news is this: while it may seem that the enemy has the upper hand, God is still on His throne. God still rules. He is still in control. He does not allow the enemy to test us beyond our limits and in every trial and temptation He is there empowering us to overcome if we let Him. So if you feel entrapped by trial and temptation, ask your Heavenly Father to show you His escape route and follow Him out into a new day of freedom!

Vindication

> *Don't hit back; discover beauty in everyone. If you've got it in you, get along with everybody. Don't insist on getting even; that's not for you to do. "I'll do the judging," says God. "I'll take care of it."*
>
> ROMANS 12:17–19

One of the hardest challenges a person can have is when they are unjustly and cruelly treated by another, either verbally, physically, materially or spiritually. When others trash our reputations behind our backs or abuse us to our faces it is hard not to retaliate there and then or to fantasize about revenge thereafter. But the Bible teaches us a different way. We can either react in the flesh or respond in the Spirit. Reacting in the flesh involves us trying to orchestrate our own vindication by getting our own back for the injustices we've received. Responding in the Spirit means doing what Jesus asks us to do, which is to bless those who curse us. It means doing what the Apostle Paul tells us here, which is to try and see the beauty within those who are doing ugly things to us. It means trusting in God that He will do the judging and that He will take care of the business of vindication. If you need vindication, let God do it. In the meantime, don't try to get even. If you've got it in you, just try to get along.

Waiting

> *It won't be long now, he's on the way;*
> *he'll show up most any minute.*
>
> HEBREWS 10:36

When a person calls for an ambulance, there is always a gap of time between the request and the answer. Sometimes it can even take longer than we would like for the rescue services to arrive. The same is true in our relationship with God. There is often a gap in time between asking God to help us and His help arriving. What do we do in the time between asking and receiving? The Bible tells us that this is the time of "waiting." Waiting in the Bible is not a passive or a negative thing. It is a process in which we actively hold fast to the promises of God and declare that what we do not yet see will become a reality in our lives. In Hebrews ten, the writer calls this "sticking it out," "staying with God's plan," and "not cutting and running." If you are living between the asking and receiving, ask God to increase your capacity for confident and creative waiting. The waiting time is a time of growth and opportunity. Those that wait upon the Lord get fresh strength (Isaiah 40). They revel in the knowledge that help is on the way.

Wisdom

> *If you don't know what you're doing,*
> *pray to the Father. He loves to help.*
>
> **JAMES 1:5**

Another translation of this verse says, "If any of you lacks wisdom, let him ask God." Wisdom is the God-given ability to know what to do, how to do it and when it needs to be done. In this sense, wisdom is the practical application of biblical principles in our everyday lives. It is the capacity to live in such a way that we reign in life even in the smallest choices and circumstances. For that to happen, we need daily to let go of our own wisdom, which is so often based on manmade philosophies and mindsets, and instead come humbly before our Heavenly Father and pray, "Father, I need your wisdom on this matter. Teach me what to do, how to do it, and when it needs to be done." We have a Father who, according to James, "loves to help." He is just waiting to be asked. When we approach Him like a child, He tells us what we need to do, helping us to understand His ways. This leads us to do the right thing with the right people at the right time. Who does not need God's glorious wisdom?

Work

> *God will order a blessing on your barns and workplaces; he'll bless you in the land that God, your God, is giving you.*
> DEUTERONOMY 28:8

Have you ever thought of God wanting to bless your workplace? Many Christians don't understand that God is not restricted to the four walls of a church building. He is the limitless Father whose presence and rule is extending over all the earth, including in workplaces. For those who hear and obey God, there are some fantastic promises in the Bible relating to the workplace. This one from Deuteronomy 28 is a promise about the blessings of God "on your barns and workplaces." It doesn't matter how irreligious your workplace is, once you're present the dynamics have already changed. You carry the presence of God. Whether your unbelieving colleagues know it yet or not is irrelevant. As a carrier of the blessings of God you are a culture shaper. You are bringing the kingdom of heaven to earth in your workplace. The moment you walk in, the moment you say a silent prayer, the atmosphere is transformed. Because you're there, God's going to fill the barns and bless the workplaces; everywhere you walk you will leave an imprint of the Father's blessing.

Youthfulness

*He renews your youth—you're
always young in his presence.*
PSALM 103:5

Do you know how you can tell if an older person knows and loves the Lord? It's because they look way younger than they really are! The simple reason for this is not because they have been applying the latest, highly expensive, anti-aging cosmetics. No, their solution is far less expensive. In fact it is entirely free! Old people who look wonderfully young and energetic have not been spending time in front of the mirror or at the gym. They have been spending time in the refreshing, invigorating, energizing presence of the Living God. You can see it in their eyes! They sparkle with life. Their hearts have a passion and a joy that many young people would covet. The wonderful thing about being in love with God is that you are never really retired. You are only re-fired. Every day the fire of God's love ignites our hearts, giving us the endless capacity to live, love and laugh. Don't rely on creams or treadmills to keep you young. It is God who renews our youth. In His presence, we are always young!

Zeal

Don't burn out; keep yourselves fueled and aflame.

ROMANS 12:11

Another version of the Bible tells us never to be lacking in zeal. Zeal is an old-fashioned word. You tend not to hear it much, except in negative statements about someone being "over-zealous," or such and such a political activist being a "zealot." But zeal in the Bible is a common theme and positive virtue. As Christians, we need zeal. We need to take responsibility to keep the fire burning in our hearts. We need to stay in love with Jesus, not losing our first love. This is not always easy. Life is sometimes harsh and demanding. Ministry can be the same, sometimes worse. In such situations, we need to take responsibility for our own soul-care and make sure that we don't become fatigued and frustrated. We really have two choices: to keep on fire or become burned out. The Father's intention is not that we should burn out but burn bright. So steward your passion for the Lord with diligence. As John Wesley once said, if we catch fire, people will come from all around to watch us burn.

My Personal Scriptures